25 Years of the Protocol on Environmental Protection to the Antarctic Treaty

COMMITTEE FOR ENVIRONMENTAL
PROTECTION

25 Years of the Protocol on Environmental Protection to the Antarctic Treaty

Secretariat of the Antarctic Treaty

Buenos Aires

2016

Published by:

Secretariat of the Antarctic Treaty

Secrétariat du Traité sur l'Antarctique

Секретариат Договора об Антарктике

Secretaría del Tratado Antártico

Maipú 757, Piso 4
C1006ACI Ciudad Autónoma
Buenos Aires - Argentina
Tel: +54 11 4320 4260
Fax: +54 11 4320 4253

ISBN 978-987-4024-10-7

Contents

Antarctica: a natural reserve, devoted to peace and science — 7

The emergence of the Madrid Protocol — 7

The Madrid Protocol — 8

The Committee for Environmental Protection. Its role and working procedure — 12

The work of the CEP — 14

Additional Reading — 18

   Table 1. Members and Observers of the Committee for Environmental Protection (as at April 2016) — 19

Antarctica: a natural reserve, devoted to peace and science

The Protocol on Environmental Protection to the Antarctic Treaty is the international agreement that establishes the framework for comprehensive protection of the Antarctic environment. It is commonly referred to as the Madrid Protocol.

The emergence of the Madrid Protocol

The Madrid Protocol was negotiated by the parties to the Antarctic Treaty between 1989 and 1991, following the failure to agree on an international regulatory instrument governing mining in Antarctica (the Convention on the Regulation of Antarctic Mineral Resource Activities, or CRAMRA).

The adoption of the Madrid Protocol includes an indefinite prohibition on any activity relating to mineral resources, other than scientific research.

The Protocol built on a range of environmental provisions agreed at several Antarctic Treaty Consultative Meetings (ATCM) since the signing of the Treaty including the 1964 Agreed Measures on the Conservation of Antarctic Fauna and Flora. It also picked up environmental management elements that had been developed during the CRAMRA negotiations (such as emergency response provisions), as well as previous work of the Scientific Committee of Antarctic Research (SCAR) and the International Maritime Organization (IMO), on waste management and marine pollution, respectively.

The Protocol was opened for signature on 4 October 1991. It entered into force on 14 January 1998.

Committee for Environmental Protection

The original 26 nations to sign the Madrid Protocol have now been joined by a further 11 nations (see Table 1).

The Madrid Protocol

The Madrid Protocol was carefully designed. Its status as a Protocol to the Antarctic Treaty was intended to strengthen the Treaty as the governance framework for the region. As such the Protocol applies also to the Antarctic Treaty area, that is, the area south of 60° South Latitude.

The Madrid Protocol was designed around a core set of environmental principles (the Protocol itself), with a series of Annexes establishing more detailed rules and provisions. This approach allows for the Annexes to be updated to accommodate changes in environmental awareness and management practices, and for additional annexes to be added as the need arises.

The central principles of the Protocol are:

- The designation of Antarctica as a 'natural reserve, devoted to peace and science';
- A prohibition on mining and mineral resource activities in the Antarctic Treaty area;
- The requirement that protection of the environment shall be a fundamental consideration in the planning and conduct of all activities in the Antarctic;
- A comprehensive framework for assessing environmental impacts in Antarctica, including prior assessment of all activities;
- A requirement to establish contingency plans and provide for prompt and effective response to environmental emergencies in the Antarctic; and

- The establishment of the Committee for Environmental Protection (CEP).

The preamble to the Madrid Protocol outlines the desire of Antarctic Treaty Parties to develop a comprehensive regime for protecting the Antarctic environment and its dependent and associated ecosystems, with benefits for all mankind.

The Madrid Protocol currently has six Annexes. These Annexes are integral to the Protocol and its legal framework. The current Annexes are:

> ANNEX I: **Environmental impact assessment** – The environmental impacts of any proposed activities in Antarctica shall, **before their commencement,** be assessed in order to: identify any impacts on the environment, including cumulative impacts; and to identify alternative potentially less harmful approaches, as well as any monitoring required to verify the predicted impacts of the activity. The extent of the environmental impact assessment required depends upon whether the predicted impacts are likely to cause less than, no more than, or more than minor or transitory impacts. Draft Comprehensive Environmental Evaluations (prepared for activities likely to have more than a minor or transitory impact) must be made publicly available, circulated to all Parties for comment and be forwarded to the CEP for consideration before the activity commences.
>
> ANNEX II: **Conservation of Antarctic fauna and flora** – Annex II provides the rules and framework for protecting animals and plants in Antarctica. Permits are required to be issued for any harmful interaction with Antarctic native species. The introduction of non-native speciesis not allowed, except for limited purposes authorised under a

permit. The Annex also provides for the designation of "Specially Protected Species". Annex II has been revised and updated in 2009, namely to consider the protection of invertebrate species.

ANNEX III: **Waste disposal and waste management** – Annex III establishes the principle that the amount of waste produced or disposed of in Antarctica should be minimised to protect the environment and other Antarctic values. It also establishes the framework for cleaning up waste sites on land generated prior to the Madrid Protocol; rules for the disposal of human waste and the use of incinerators; and a requirement to develop waste management plans. Some products, such as Polychlorinated biphenyls (PCBs), polystyrene packaging beads and pesticides, are prohibited in the Antarctic.

ANNEX IV: **Prevention of marine pollution** – Annex IV prohibits the discharge of noxious liquid substances, plastics and other garbage to sea from ships. Its framework is broadly consistent with the International Convention for the Prevention of Pollution from Ships, 1973 as modified by the Protocol of 1978 (MARPOL). The Annex also requires Antarctic Treaty Parties to prepare contingency plans for marine pollution emergencies in the Antarctic Treaty area.

Annexes I to IV were adopted in 1991 together with the Protocol and entered into force in 1998.

ANNEX V: **Management of protected areas** – Annex V establishes two forms of protected area (Antarctic Specially Protected Areas (ASPAs) and Antarctic Specially Managed Areas (ASMAs). Both ASPAs and ASMAs require management plans to be prepared, which must be reviewed at least every five years. ASPAs are designated to manage and "protect outstanding environmental, scientific, historic, aesthetic or wilderness values" and scientific research. Permits are required to enter and conduct activities in ASPAs. ASMAs are designated to "...assist in the planning and co-ordination of activities, avoid possible conflicts, improve cooperation between Parties or minimise environmental impacts". Annex V also provides for the designation of Historic Sites or Monuments to protect and conserve sites of recognised historic value. Annex V was adopted in 1991 and entered into force in 2002.

ANNEX VI: **Liability for environmental emergencies** – This Annex outlines arrangements to prevent and respond to environmental emergencies in the Antarctic Treaty area arising from scientific research programmes, tourism and other governmental and non-governmental activities. It establishes the rules governing liability for environmental emergencies, and provides that compensation may be claimed from the polluter if that party has not taken prompt and effective response action.

Annex VI on Liability Arising from Environmental Emergencies was adopted in 2005 and will enter into force once approved by all Consultative Parties.

Negotiation of and agreement on the Madrid Protocol constituted the culmination of years of development of environmental standards and practices, which were synthesized and articulated into a single comprehensive agreement. The Protocol set out new rules on environmental protection, including new restrictions to human activity in Antarctica and a framework to incorporate new issues through the elaboration of additional annexes. Through the Protocol, the protection of the Antarctic environment was established as the third pillar of the Antarctic Treaty, together with peaceful use and international scientific cooperation.

The Committee for Environmental Protection. Its role and working procedure

The Committee for Environmental Protection is established under Article 11 of the Madrid Protocol. The Committee's role is to provide advice and formulate recommendations to the Antarctic Treaty Consultative Parties "in connection with the implementation of" the Madrid Protocol.

Article 12 of the Madrid Protocol outlines the remit of the Committee, which comprises the advice on the effectiveness of measures taken pursuant to the Protocol and the need to update, strengthen or improve such measures, including the need for additional Annexes. The CEP's functions also include providing advice on a variety of issues, such as:

- the effectiveness of measures taken pursuant to the Protocol;
- the need to update, strengthen or improve such measures;
- the need for additional measures, including the need for additional Annexes;
- the application and implementation of the environmental impact assessment procedures;
- means of minimising or mitigating environmental impacts of activities in the Antarctic Treaty area;
- procedures for situations requiring urgent action, including response action in environmental emergencies;
- the operation and development of a Protected Area system in the Antarctic;
- inspection procedures;

- the collection, archiving, exchange and evaluation of information related to environmental protection;

- the state of the Antarctic environment; and

- the need for scientific research, including environmental monitoring, related to the implementation of the Madrid Protocol.

Once the Protocol was ratified, the CEP got quickly into business, much helped by the ATCMs maintaining a Transitional Environmental Working Group (TEWG) from 1995 to do preparatory work prior to CEP's establishment.

The Committee for Environmental Protection has met annually since 1998, usually in conjunction with the Antarctic Treaty Consultative Meeting. Parties to the Protocol are entitled to be members of the Committee and to participate in decision-making. Any Contracting Party to the Antarctic Treaty that is not a party to the Protocol is entitled to send an observer to the Meetings of the Committee. The Scientific Committee on Antarctic Research (SCAR), the Commission for the Conservation of Antarctic Marine Living Resources (CCAMLR) and the Council of Managers of National Antarctic Programmes (COMNAP) attend the Committee as observers. In addition, with the agreement of the Antarctic Treaty Consultative Meeting, the Committee is able to invite other relevant experts and organisations (see Table 1).

The Committee for Environmental Protection has its own rules of procedure, and their meetings are conducted in the four official languages of the Antarctic Treaty (English, French, Russian and Spanish).

The Committee provides a report of its meeting to the Antarctic Treaty Consultative Meeting, which in turn considers the report and any recommendations.

Committee for Environmental Protection

The work of the CEP

Since its first meeting in Tromso in 1998, the year the Protocol came into force, the Committee for Environmental Protection has regularly provided advice to the Antarctic Treaty Consultative Meeting and built a considerable body of work. This has included the elaboration of numerous practical environmental management tools on issues such as Environmental Impact Assessment, protected areas, conservation of flora and fauna, environmental monitoring, marine pollution, specially protected species, wastes from past activities, historic sites and monuments, non-native species, among other issues.

All these guidelines and procedures for protecting the Antarctic environment have been consolidated in the "CEP Handbook", which is kept periodically updated in the ATS website. The Handbook consolidates much of the substantive work of the Committee, in the form of guidelines and procedures for protecting the Antarctic environment. This work covers, among many other things:

- Guidelines for Environmental Impact Assessment in Antarctica and procedures for intersessional consideration of draft Comprehensive Environmental Evaluations
- Procedures and guidelines for the designation of Antarctic protected areas, and the preparation and consideration of Management Plans for these areas
- Guidelines for the operation of aircraft near birds colonies in Antarctica
- Guidelines for consideration of proposals for to designate Specially Protected Species
- An Antarctic clean-up manual for waste and abandoned places

- An manual containing guidance for non-native species prevention, monitoring and response
- Guidelines for dealing with ballast water the Antarctic Treaty area
- A Checklist for inspections of Antarctic Specially Protected Areas and Antarctic Specially Managed Areas
- General guidelines for visitors to the Antarctic; and
- Practical guidelines for environmental monitoring in Antarctica

The CEP's advice to the ATCM has led to the adoption of a number of measures regulating human activities in Antarctica. More than 40% of the over one hundred of Measures, Decisions and Resolutions adopted by the ATCM since the Protocol entered into force have stemmed from the work of the Committee.

This reflects the high priority the Antarctic Treaty Parties place on continually enhancing the international framework of policy and law for the comprehensive environmental protection of the Antarctic.

The work of the CEP is not limited to its annual meetings, but extends to the whole year through intersessional activities. Such activities include the open-ended intersessional contact groups (ICGs) established to undertake specific complex or time-consuming work that cannot be completed during the Committee meetings; the conduct of informal discussions for ease of access to the dialogue on a number of issues brought up during the meeting; and the work of the Subsidiary Group on Management Plans (SGMP), which routinely undertake the consideration of new and revised management plans for Antarctic specially protected or specially managed areas. Finally, the consideration of certain types of environmental impact assessments (Comprehensive Environmental Evaluations) is also undertaken intersessionally.

Committee for Environmental Protection

Since the inception of the CEP, over 90 intersessional activities have been carried out. Firstly, these took place through e-mail exchanges. Since 2005 the Committee has utilised a web-based discussion forum, which provides an open and dynamic environment for intersessional work, and creates a very valuable archive of such discussions. In addition, databases on EIA documents and on the protected area system were prepared and are hosted in the ATS website to assist the work of the CEP members and for public information.

The CEP has also organised a series of workshops to address particular issues. These have addressed issues such as: Antarctic protected areas (Lima, 1999), Antarctica's Future Environmental Challenges (Edinburgh, 2006), and Marine and Terrestrial Antarctic Specially Managed Areas (Montevideo, 2011). In addition, two Joint Workshops (Baltimore, 2009 and Punta Arenas, 2016) have been held to identify areas of common interest and to develop a shared understanding of the conservation objectives and priorities between the CEP and the Scientific Committee of CAMLR.

From a workshop held in 2006, a proposal was formulated to prepare a five-year rolling work plan to guide the Committee's work, recognising that some issues demanded more immediate attention than others. The first five-year work plan was adopted in 2008, and it is revised each year to reflect Members' agreed priorities. The rolling five-year work plan provides the Committee for Environmental Protection with, not only a framework for considering current issues, but for anticipating future challenges.

The 2015 plan gives high priority to work in the following areas:

- Addressing the risks associated with the introduction of species not native to in the Antarctic, and the transfer of native species within Antarctica.

- Appropriately managing the environmental impacts of tourism and non-governmental activities.
- Understanding and responding to the environmental consequences climate change in the Antarctic region.
- Improving the effectiveness of protected area management, and further developing the Antarctic protected area system, including in the marine environment.

The CEP's five year work plan provides the ATCM with an opportunity to comment on and influence the prioritization of the CEP's work in accordance with the ATCM's own interests and priorities, and allows the CEP's observers and invited experts to see in advance when the CEP is likely to tackle issues in which they have an interest and thus plan their own contributions to the CEP's work.

Since its first Meeting, the workload and diversity of issues considered by the CEP has increased. The Parties maintain their continuing strong commitment to protecting the Antarctic environment, and to addressing new and emerging challenges presented by human activities in the Antarctic region, by climate change, and by other pressures originating in other parts of the globe. Protection of the Antarctic environment, and its dependent and related ecosystems, will remain the highest priority of the Antarctic Treaty system. The Madrid Protocol, and the Committee for Environmental Protection are fundamental to maintaining Antarctica as a natural reserve, devoted to peace and science.

Committee for Environmental Protection

Additional Reading[1]

Protocol on Environmental Protection to the Antarctic Treaty

- Annex I Environmental Impact Assessment
- Annex II Conservation of Antarctic Fauna and Flora
- Annex III Waste Disposal and Waste Management
- Annex IV Prevention of Marine Pollution
- Annex V Area Protection and Management
- Annex VI Liability Arising from Environmental Emergencies

Committee for Environmental Protection Handbook

Environmental Impact Assessment Database

Antarctic Protected Areas Database

---

[1] Available at http://www.ats.aq

Table 1. Members and Observers of the Committee for Environmental Protection (as at April 2016)

Members – Parties to the Madrid Protocol*			
Argentina	Australia	Belarus	Belgium
Brazil	Bulgaria	Canada	Chile
China	Czech Republic	Ecuador	Finland
France	Germany	Greece	India
Italy	Japan	Korea (RoK)	Monaco
Netherlands	New Zealand	Norway	Pakistan
Peru	Poland	Portugal	Romania
Russian Federation	South Africa	Spain	Sweden
Ukraine	United Kingdom	United States	Uruguay
Venezuela			
Observers – Parties to the Antarctic Treaty that are not party to the Madrid Protocol			
Austria	Colombia	Cuba	Denmark
Estonia	Guatemala	Hungary	Iceland
Kazakhstan	Korea (DPRK)	Malaysia	Mongolia
Papua New Guinea	Slovak Republic	Switzerland	Turkey

Table 1. (Cont.)

Observers – Organisations identified in the Madrid Protocol and/or Rules of Procedure			
Scientific Committee on Antarctic Research (SCAR)	Scientific Committee for the Conservation of Antarctic Marine Living Resources (SC-CAMLR)	Council of Managers of National Antarctic Programs (COMNAP)	
Experts – Other scientific, environmental and technical organisations			
Antarctic and Southern Ocean Coalition (ASOC)	International Association of Antarctica Tour Operations (IAATO)	International Hydrographic Organization (IHO)	International Union for the Conservation of Nature (IUCN)
United Nations Environment Programme (UNEP)	World Meteorological Organization (WMO)		

*A current list is available at
http://www.ats.aq/devAS/ats_parties.aspx?lang=e